WHAT WE CAN DO ABOUT

WASTING WATER

Donna Bailey

PENNYCOOK SCHOOL

VALLEJO, CALIFORNIA

WHAT WE CAN DO ABOUT

WASTING WATER

Donna Bailey

Franklin Watts

New York   London   Toronto   Sydney

© 1991 Franklin Watts

Franklin Watts
387 Park Avenue South
New York, NY 10016

Design: Julian Holland Publishing Ltd.
Illustrator: Tony Gibbons
Picture Research: Alison Renwick

Printed in Italy

Library of Congress Cataloging-in-Publication Data
Bailey, Donna
    Wasting water / Donna Bailey.
        p.   cm. — (What we can do about)
    Includes index.
    Summary: Discusses how water is wasted and how it can be conserved and used
more effectively.
    ISBN 0-531-11019-2
    1. Water — Waste — Juvenile literature. 2. Water conservation — Juvenile
literature. (1. Water conservation. 2. Conservation of natural resources.)
I. Title II. Series.
TD495 B35   1991
333.91'137 — dc20   91-8657
                                                                         CIP
                                                                          AC

Photograph acknowledgements
t = top b = bottom
Cover: Walter Rawlings/Robert Harding Picture Library, pp6 Shulke/Planet Earth
Pictures, 9 J Allan Cash Photo Library, 10t Chris Fairclough Colour Library, 10b J
Allan Cash Photo Library, 12t Chris Fairclough Colour Library, 12b Eric Crighton/
Bruce Coleman Limited, 13 Chris Fairclough Colour Library, 15t C Macpherson/
The Environmental Picture Library, 15b J Allan Cash Photo Library, 16t Jaroslav
Poncar/Bruce Coleman Limited, 16b Alan Carr/Robert Harding Picture Library, 18
J Allan Cash Photo Library, 19 Dave Jacobs/Robert Harding Picture Library, 20
Robert Harding Picture Library, 21 Richard Matthews/Planet Earth Pictures, 22,
25 Robert Harding Picture Library, 26 Kaiser/Greenpeace Communications
Limited.

Contents

Water on Earth

Photographs of Earth from space show that, beneath a layer of swirling clouds, oceans cover about 70 percent of the earth's surface.

Although there is so much water on Earth, most of it is salty and cannot be used for drinking. Only about 4 percent is fresh water.

The diagram below shows how fresh water is made during the **water cycle**. Warmth from the sun **evaporates** water from the rivers and sea, producing a gas known as water vapor. The water vapor rises, and **condenses** into water droplets which make mist and clouds. Winds carry the clouds over the land, and the fresh water falls as rain. The rain runs off into streams and rivers which flow back to the sea. Some of the rainwater soaks through the soil and joins the **groundwater** stored in cracks and spaces in rocks.

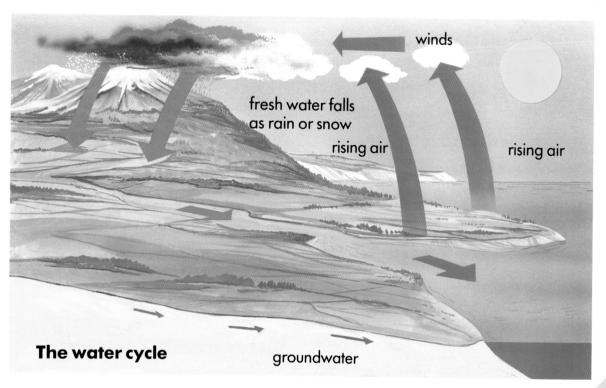

winds

fresh water falls as rain or snow

rising air

rising air

The water cycle

groundwater

A growing demand for water

We all need at least one liter (1 qt) of drinking water a day to keep us alive. We also use water for cooking, for washing ourselves, for washing our clothes and cars, to flush the toilet and to water our plants. In fact, every American uses about 300 l (80 gal) of water a day. If we add the water used by industry and farming every day, the figure is much higher.

Throughout the world, the amount of rain which falls each year remains about the same, so there is the same amount of water available. However, the demand for water is growing. This is partly because the number of people in the world continues to grow, and partly because people now expect a better standard of living.

Daily use of water per person

toilet flushing
102 l (27 gal)

washing machine
64 l (17 gal)

showers
53 l (14 gal)

faucets   38 l (10 gal)

baths   30 l (8 gal)

dishwashing   8 l (2 gal)

Total use per day

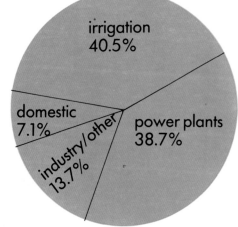

irrigation
40.5%

domestic
7.1%

industry/other
13.7%

power plants
38.7%

In some countries people may not have running water in their homes. They must be careful about the water they use. They collect the water they need for washing and cooking from the village well. In other countries people do not worry about how much water they use. Dishwashers and washing machines save them the effort of washing plates and clothes by hand, but these machines use a lot more water. Farmers need more water to grow more crops. Factories need more water to produce more goods. One way in which we can all help to make sure there is enough water for everyone is to use water wisely and not to waste it.

Avoiding waste

Imagine that the water supply to your home has been cut and you have to collect all the water you need from a well or **standpipe**. How would you use that water once you had carried it home?

Try to think how you and your family can avoid wasting water. For example, do not wash your hands or brush your teeth under a running tap. When you use a tap, make sure you turn it off properly. Dripping taps can waste a lot of water.

Whenever possible, take a shower instead of a bath. By doing this you could save about 60 l (16 gal) of water. If you do have a bath, keep the water shallow and think whether the water could be reused. Some people use their bath and dish-washing water to water the garden.

If you need to wash something urgently, either do it by hand or make sure there is enough washing to make a full load for the washing machine. Some machines use as much as 178 l (47 gal) of water per wash. Other machines have a half-load program. This not only saves water but also saves detergent.

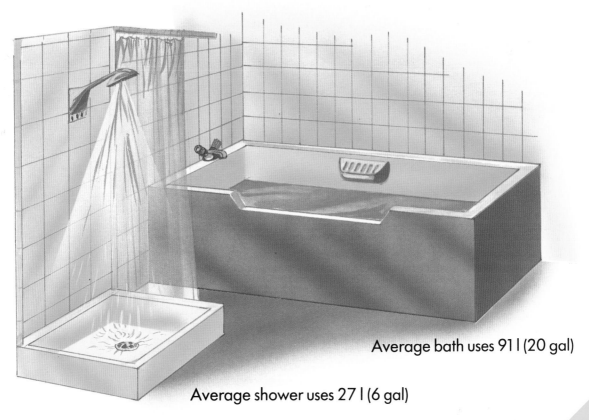

Average bath uses 91 l (20 gal)

Average shower uses 27 l (6 gal)

Saving water outside

You do not need to use tap water for watering plants or for washing the car. If your family has a rainwater tank which collects the water that runs off the roof, use this water instead. If not, you could always collect some rainwater in buckets or bowls. After you have washed your hair, give it a final rinse with some of the rainwater you have collected. It will leave your hair soft and shiny.

People often leave hoses on for longer than is needed, and waste water. For many small gardens it is not really necessary to use a hose and sprinkler. Use a watering can instead. With a watering can you can make sure the water goes only where it is needed and none is wasted.

Watering the garden with a sprinkler is a very wasteful use of water. In dry weather or during a drought other people may not have enough water for their everyday needs.

When cars get dirty, people like to wash and polish them. Some people take their cars to a car wash. Other people wash their cars every weekend, using a hose to spray water over the car before they polish it. Washing the car with a hose may use much less water than the car wash, but a lot of water is still wasted.

If you use a bucket and sponge when you wash the car, it will make the car just as clean and will waste much less water.

Using less water

Instead of wasting water we should all think of ways in which we can use less water. An average toilet flushes 14 l (3.7 gal) of water. Half of this water could be saved by installing a twin system flush which allows a choice of half or full flush. Toilets which flush only 6 l (1.6 gal) or even 4 l (1 gal) are now available.

Even without installing a new flush system, most toilets can be made to use less water by putting a brick in the cistern. The brick should be clean, and put into the cistern away from the valve and ballcock. The brick takes up space so that less water is needed to refill the cistern each time the toilet is flushed.

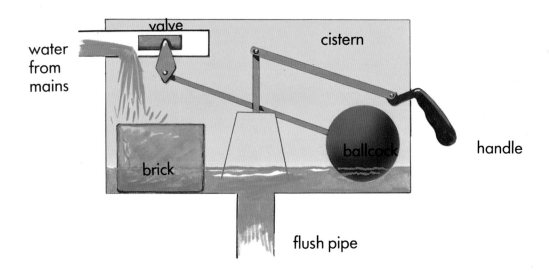

water from mains

valve

cistern

brick

ballcock

handle

flush pipe

A dishwasher needs about 50 l (13 gal) of water every time it is used, a lot more than washing-up by hand. Perhaps you could help save water by offering to do the washing-up by hand instead.

If you notice a dripping tap at home, tell your parents so that it can be mended as soon as possible. Broken water pipes or **mains** should be reported to the water authority.

Water for farming

Farmers use a lot of water for their animals and for their crops. For example, it takes 113 l (300 gal) of water to produce one loaf of bread and almost 1,500 l (4,000 gal) of water to raise each pound of beef. When there is not enough water, the grass dries out and the cattle get thin and weak.

All plants need water to grow. In the summer when there is not much rain, some farmers **irrigate** their fields by spraying water over the crops. Spray irrigation is very wasteful because so much of the water evaporates, sometimes before it reaches the ground.

In very dry countries farmers irrigate their fields with water from underground storage tanks or rivers. The water is led through ditches to the fields where it is needed.

Some crops need more water than others. For example, 1 kg (2 lb) of rice needs about 4,500 l (1,189 gal) of water from the time it is planted until it is harvested. Farmers plant the rice seedlings in fields which they flood with water from nearby rivers and streams.

When farmers take too much water from rivers, then lakes and seas may dry up. This has happened in central Asia where farmers have taken so much water to irrigate their cotton fields that the rivers that flow into the Aral Sea often run dry before they reach it. As a result the Aral Sea has lost 69 percent of its water and is now less than half its original size. The shrinking of the sea has killed nearly all the wildlife, especially the fish which were once plentiful.

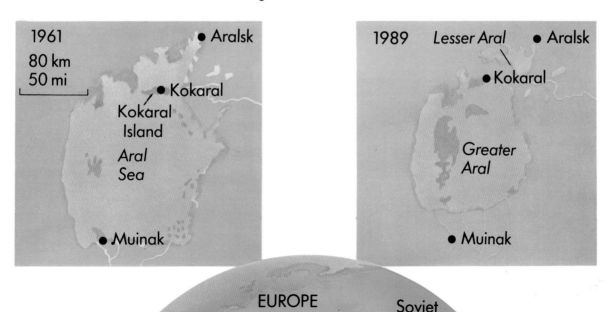

1961
80 km
50 mi
● Aralsk
● Kokaral
Kokaral
Island
Aral
Sea
● Muinak

1989 Lesser Aral ● Aralsk
● Kokaral
Greater
Aral
● Muinak

EUROPE
Soviet
Union

Water for industry

The paper industry is one of the largest industrial users of water. It needs enormous amounts of water every day. Our picture shows the dirty water from a paper factory. The water is being cleaned before it is put back into the river.

Power plants that burn oil or coal use millions of gallons of water every hour. The water is heated to produce steam which turns the **generators** that make the electricity. Water is also used to cool the steam so that it condenses back into water which can be reused.

Hydroelectric power plants use water stored behind dams to make electricity. In the building at the base of the dam in the picture, water from the lake is used to push against blades inside a **turbine**. This makes the blades spin around. The turbine drives a generator that makes the electricity. The water used to turn the turbines then flows back into the river.

Supply and demand

In some countries, such as Norway and Canada, there are many rivers and lakes. These countries are able to obtain most of their water from these surface sources. In other countries, such as the United States and Britain, much of the water comes from the ground. Underground rocks which contain stores of water are called **aquifers**. Sometimes water from aquifers flows out of the ground naturally as springs and streams. When water does not come to the surface by itself, **boreholes** may be dug to reach the aquifers. Water is then pumped up from the aquifer to the surface.

As we take more and more water from deeper boreholes, the amount of water stored in the aquifers falls. Springs dry up and the source of a river moves downhill. When this happens, riverside wetlands may also dry up and an entire **habitat**, once home to water birds and plants, disappears.

In order to control water supplies, so that enough is available when and where it is needed, artificial lakes, or **reservoirs**, may be built. Dams are constructed across river valleys, and the rain and river water collect behind the dam. The water can be drained from the reservoir when demand is high.

Sometimes attractive countryside and important wildlife sites are lost when another reservoir has to be built to meet the demand for more water.

Clean water

Thousands of years ago, the Romans were the first people to build **aqueducts** so that they could bring water from distant rivers and lakes to the cities. Our picture shows the Pont du Gard, an aqueduct in France. The water was carried above the top row of arches.

In the past, people also took their water direct from springs, rivers and lakes. Others dug wells and lifted the water in buckets or by hand pump. In either case, people had to live near a supply of water or walk long distances to get water as they still do in parts of the world today.

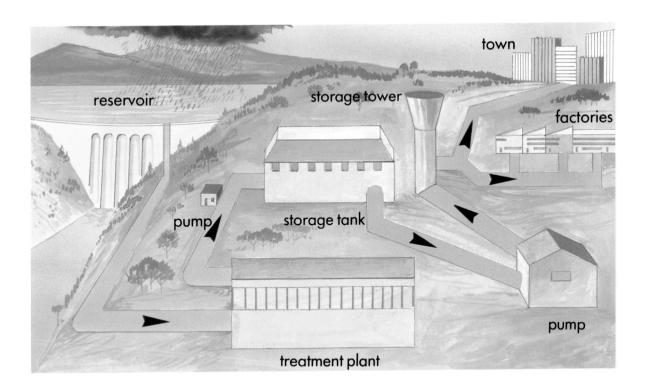

reservoir · storage tower · town · factories · pump · storage tank · treatment plant · pump

Water companies pipe water from rivers, boreholes and reservoirs to **treatment plants** where the water is cleaned. In the treatment plants, the water passes through screens just like sieves to remove any floating material. Chemicals are added to the water to kill **bacteria** and **microorganisms**. The clean water is then pumped to storage tanks or towers. When it is needed, the water is pumped along pipelines to people's homes.

All the water pumped to our homes is treated so that it is pure enough to drink. Yet 90 percent of this clean water is flushed down the toilet or used to wash dishes, clothes and cars.

Down the drain!

Waste water from our homes, offices, factories, farms and streets is called **sewage**. Sewage travels through a network of drains and pipes to the sewage treatment plant. At the treatment plant, the waste water is cleaned. The cleaned water, known as **effluent**, is usually put back into the rivers. Water may be taken from and returned to the same river several times along its length.

open channels where grit and sand are removed

sludge

screens

sedimentation tanks

liquid sewage flows along pipes which lead into the sprinkler arms

filter tanks

liquid sewage is sprayed over the filter tanks by slowly rotating sprinkler arms

effluent

Sewage arriving at the sewage treatment plant is almost all water. At the plant, the sewage is first passed through screens to take out pieces of rags, plastic, wood and other materials. It then flows slowly along open channels where grit and sand are taken out, before it goes to the **sedimentation tanks** like those in our picture. The solid matter in the sewage sinks to the bottom of these tanks and is removed as **sludge**. The liquid sewage is sprayed over circular filter tanks. In these tanks organic matter such as fats or soap is taken out. The effluent then flows out into the river.

In Eastern Europe much of the water used in industry contains poisonous chemicals. The factories pour their untreated water directly into rivers which then become heavily **polluted**.

We should all be careful about what we pour into water, as polluted water is often wasted water. Oil and grease can be recycled, and should not be poured down drains. When possible use "environmentally friendly" detergents and cleaners. These contain fewer of the chemicals that pollute waste water, making it difficult to treat.

Activities

1 Ask your family to help you make a survey of water use in your home over a weekend.

Ask them to note down when they wash clothes and dishes and take a bath or a shower.

At the end of the weekend, check the list and think of ways that you and your family could use less water.

2 Ask your parents or teacher if you can make a survey at your local car wash.

Count the number of cars that are washed in one hour. Write to the owner of the car wash and ask how much water is used to wash one car. Work out how many cars could be washed using that same amount of water and a bucket and sponge.

Water use survey		
	Saturday	Sunday
Washing machine	10·00am	
Dishwasher	9·00am 2·00pm 8·30pm	
Washing up by hand		
Bath		
Shower		

Glossary

aqueduct: a water-carrying channel which crosses a valley, usually by means of a bridge.

aquifer: underground rock, sand, or gravel that water can seep through, and where water can be stored.

bacteria: tiny creatures that can only be seen with a strong microscope. Some are harmful and cause disease. Others are useful and break down dead plants and animals.

borehole: a well sunk deep into rock, from which water is pumped to the surface.

condense: to become more dense or thickly crowded together, e.g. when water vapor condenses, the small particles that make up the vapor crowd together and form liquid water.

effluent: 1 Water that is put back into a river after it has been cleaned at a sewage plant. **2** Liquid waste from a factory.

evaporate: to change into vapor.

generator: a machine that makes electricity.

groundwater: underground water held in cracks and spaces in rocks.

habitat: the natural home of a plant or animal.

hydroelectricity: electricity that is made using the power of falling water.

irrigate: to water crops, through a system of underground pipes, ditches, or by spraying.

mains: the pipes that supply water to towns or houses.

microorganisms: tiny bacteria, animals and plants which can only be seen with a microscope.

pollute: to dirty or poison the air, land or water.

reservoir: a place where water is collected and stored.

sedimentation tanks: large containers which allow solid matter in sewage to settle on the bottom.

sewage: waste matter from houses, factories, farms, streets and offices that is carried away in pipes.

sludge: the solid matter which is separated out during the treatment of sewage.

standpipe: a tap in the street where people can collect water in buckets or other containers.

treatment plant: a place where water is cleaned before it is supplied to houses.

turbine: a wheel with many curved blades which spin around rapidly when water pushes against them.

water cycle: the endless process in which rain falls, is turned into vapor by the heat of the sun, rises, turns into droplets, and falls back to earth.

Index